THE COMPLETE
BIBLE WORKBOOK
FOR FINANCIAL BUDGETING

Lovell Brown

Published and Distributed by:
Superb Publishing House
Los Angeles, California
Superbpublishing@gmail.com

Packaging/Consulting
Professional Publishing House
1425 W. Manchester Ave. Ste. B
Los Angeles, California 90047
323-750-3592
Email: professionalpublishinghouse@yahoo.com
www.Professionalpublishinghouse.com

Cover design: TWA Solutions
First printing March 2020
978-0-578-71129-4
10987654321

Acknowledgments

First, I want to thank God, the Creator, for giving me the wisdom and insight to create this book. Without the faith and spiritual power, I could not have done it. From the bottom of my heart, God, I thank You.

I want to thank my mother, Curtis Mae Robinson, and my dad, the late Cliffton Brown—rest in peace. Thank you for providing emotional and physical care for me.

Thanks to my three young adult children: Levinia, Levonea and Lovell, Jr., who are the lights of my life. I thank you for being great, productive citizens.

Thanks to my sister, Clara, for her spiritual wisdom.

Thanks to my two nieces: Latrice and Brenda for encouraging me to stay strong through all my unforeseen obstacles.

Thanks to my oldest brother, the late James Robinson, rest in peace; without you, I would not have become the man I am today.

Thanks to my other sisters and two brothers: Brenda, Gina, Michelle, Debra, Eric, and Tony. We grew up together in the same household and we were very poor. Society said we would be in jail and we would not amount to anything. I thank God, we all made it through.

I give special thanks to my brother, Eric, who reminded me during the times we were in foster care that we could accomplish anything we wanted to.

Thanks to my first cousin and their mother, Auntie Juanita, Ted, rest in peace. Thanks to Jackie, Sandra, and Michael for your continued prayer.

Thanks to my nieces and nephews, which are too many to list; I love you all. Keep up the good work and pursue your dreams in life.

I extend special thanks to all my friends who believed in me and who kept me in their prayers.

Thanks to Brother Trap for the motivational talks as we pushed each other for greatness.

Thanks to Mr. Stark for his support and being a friend.

Thanks to Attorney C.J. Moore and her family for keeping me in their prayers.

Thanks Mr. Ogburn for his friendship and business strategy.

Finally, I would like to express my gratitude to Dr. Rosie Milligan for encouraging me and assisting me in starting my own publishing company. You are truly the OB-GYN in the publishing industry and I thank you for helping me to birth my first "book baby."

TABLE OF CONTENTS

INTRODUCTION

The Spiritual Individual's starting point for budgeting is to have faith and begin to establish a financial plan that allows you to visualize what expenses you have. It's so simple that we sometimes ignore this basic principle. The scripture speaks of James, a servant of God and our Lord Jesus (James 1:2-4 KJV), "My brethren count it all joy when ye fall into temptation knowing this, that the trying of your faith worketh patience, but let patience have her perfect work, that ye may be perfect and entire, wanting nothing." If we try to live our financial life without God's perfect order, it can become complex. If we acknowledge our Lord Jesus Christ as Spiritual Individuals, we will truly have a prosperous life. It's common for Spiritual Individuals to face financial hardship in their lifetime, problems of saving and managing debt are the number one downfall for many individuals.

Many of our problems result from a lack of budgeting skills that affect our lives. Most Spiritual Individuals, who go deeply into debt, have no idea how much they spend on entertainment, clothing, food, or non-necessities every month. "But godliness with contentment is great gain. For we brought nothing into the world, and we can take nothing out of it. But, if we have food and clothing, we will be content with that," 1 Timothy 6:6-8 (NIV).

Although budgeting is important, there appears to be a lack of motivation in the area of being a good steward concerning your finances. God does provide instruction to become wealthy, I just don't get it. Spiritual Individuals who do not mind working to bring home a decent salary, but they somehow run out of money before the next paycheck arrives. Deuteronomy 8:17-18 (KJV) states, "And thou say in thine heart, my power and the might of mine hand hath gotten me this wealth. But thou shalt remember the Lord thy God: for it is he that giveth thee power to get wealth, that he may establish his covenant which he swore unto thy Fathers, as it is this day." All you need is faith and the ability to establish a financial budget, and that's where *The Complete Bible Workbook For Financial Budgeting* comes in.

There is stewardship of financial discipline just like money. Time can be spent or invested (Proverb 22:7 (KJV)), "Remind us that the rich ruleth over the poor and the borrower is servant to the lender." We as Spiritual Individuals need to budget and invest our money wisely in such a way to bring us financial prosperity. Proverbs 10-4 (KJV) states, "He becometh poor that dealeth with a slack hand: but the hand of the diligent maketh rich." Budgeting involves planning, accountability, and honesty.

The workbook uses scriptural references and has been designed for the committed Spiritual Individual who is ready to accept personal financial responsibility. Now take the first step toward financial budgeting by turning the page and you'll soon see how easy it is to get your finances back on track.

DISCLAIMER:

The information contained in this workbook is not intended to be a substitute for legal or financial advice that can be provided by your attorney, accountant or financial advisor.

My goal is to educate on financial budgeting, but your success depends solely on your own efforts, commitment, and dedication to put into practice what has been outlined in this workbook and your follow through.

I cannot predict that you will attain a particular result. You must understand that results are different for each individual. Good luck on your journey to financial success.

CHAPTER 1
Getting Started

"Equip yourself with the whole armor of God."

History of Money

The history of money begins with our earliest ancestor, Adam, who was placed in the garden eastward of Eden where there was a river flowing from Eden which separated into four river heads. Genesis 2:11-12, states that the name of the first river is called Pishon and it winds through the entire land of Havilah, where the origination of gold aromatic resin and onyx was there. As people evolved, they were self-sufficient, providing their own food, clothing, and shelter from their surroundings. They learned to trade in abundance for items they needed. That's how the bartering system evolved as early as 2500 B.C. Various precious metals were used to pay for goods and services in Egypt and Asia minor. By 700 B.C., the Kingdom of Lydia was minting coins made of electrum, a pale-yellow alloy of gold and silver so they wouldn't rust if stored for a long time. Matthew 6:19 (NIV) reminds us, "Do not store up for yourselves treasures on earth, where moth and rust destroy and where thieves break in and steal. But store up for yourselves treasure in heaven, where moth and rust do not destroy and where thieves do not break in and steal."

The value of money is worth whatever its purchasing power is at that time a purchase is made. Using money means that buying and selling don't have to happen at the same time. Remember as Christians, we are stewards or managers of the money God has allowed us to receive. As Christians, we own nothing. All we have belongs to the Lord. In the book of Haggai 2:8, it says, "The Lord Almighty declares the silver and gold is all mine." Now that you understand that principle, you will then be able to make God your partner.

The U.S. has a national banking system to oversee its economy and monetary policies and the Federal Reserve System is the guardian of the nation's money resources, which have twelve separate district banks with twenty-five regional branches located throughout the country. The Federal Reserve has many roles and responsibilities to keep the economy healthy. The *regulator* buys and sells government securities to maintain the value of the dollars, and there is the *banker* who maintains bank accounts for the U.S. Treasury. If a bank needs to borrow money, it can turn to the Federal Reserve Bank, and let's not forget the *auditor* who monitors the business affairs and audit the records of all of the banks in its system. Then you have the controller; when currency wears out, the federal will take it out of circulation and authorizes its replacement. Now, what do we have here? The *guardian*, which stores the gold in the New York Federal Reserve Bank. Proverbs 13:22 (NIV) gives us a very simple explanation, "And the wealth of the sinner is laid up for the righteous." Ultimately, you don't own anything. Psalm 24:1 (NIV) says, "The earth is the Lord's and everything in it, the world, and all who live in it." Remember God wants you to prosper. Remember what Matthew 6:24 (NIV) states, "No man can serve two masters either he will hate the one and love the other, or he will be devoted to the one and despise the other. You cannot serve both God and money."

Budgeting Armor

Your credit card bills, entertainment, rent, insurance, holiday gifts, birthday gifts, car payments, and non-essentials are competing for your income and making you less focused on becoming debt-free because the demand for goods and services is a priority on earth. Ecclesiastes 3:13 (NIV) states, "Every man should eat and drink and enjoy the good of all his labor; it's the gift of God." Today, many Christians are living in financial bondage with past due bills and other financial challenges that do not bring satisfaction to God. I believe that Christians must equip themselves with the whole armor of God (sword, shoes, breastplate, shield, strong belt, and helmet) to get out of financial bondage. We are engaged in an economic battle where all believers find themselves subjected to this earthly economic system, which is continuously leaving your wallet empty, but don't panic. Believe it or not, by equipping yourself with the whole armor of God, all you will need is a budget and a financial plan that will help you make the right spending decisions. Galatians 6:4 (NIV) states, "Let us not be weary in well-doing; for in dry season we shall reap, if we faint not." Accepting responsibility for taking control of your finances means taking action. The items you would need consist of pencil, stationery supplies, a file cabinet, notebook, calculator and your paycheck stub. You will need this to budget your finances no matter how many bills you have. Ecclesiastes 10:19 (NIV) states, "Money answereth all things."

A budget can help you make smarter spending decisions and more importantly, God desires that His people prosper financially. Begin today and set up your budget. Stop worrying about being able to pay your bills. If you follow God's plan, your finances will prosper. Roman 12:2 (NIV) reads, "Do not conform any longer to the pattern of this world, but be transformed by renewing of your mind. Then you will be able to test and approve what God's will is—his good, pleasing and perfect will."

Bonus Report

HOW TO COLLECT MONEY YOU KNOW NOTHING ABOUT!

Millions of Christians have money owed to them that they know nothing about. Proverbs 18-15 (NIV) states, "The heart of the discerning acquires knowledge: the ears of the wise seek it out." Many of us find it hard to believe that this money could come from forgotten bank accounts, life insurance proceeds, unclaimed inheritances, old utility deposits, unpaid tax refunds, and other sources. This is money waiting to be claimed by you if you are the direct owner or heir to this money.

This is money that has "Fallen Through the System." You changed your address or changed your name, or computers bury your file. After three to five years, the company gives up and turns the assets over to the state. The state is supposed to track you down, but most states don't make any effort. Here's how to see if there is any money waiting for you. Call the "Unclaimed Property" Division of your State's Treasurer's office and any other states where you or your family have lived. When you call, give your name, address and social security number to the Unclaimed Property agent. The agent will then check the records to see if you are due anything.

CHAPTER 2

The Right Armor
"Now it's time to prepare for budgeting."

The Right Pencil

Remember the story of Noah? In Genesis 6:14-15 (NIV), God instructed Noah to build an Ark of cypress wood; make rooms in it and coat it with pitch inside and outside, and God said, "This is how you are to build it: The ark is to be three hundred cubits long, fifty cubits wide and thirty cubits high." God also told Noah, in Genesis 6:19 that he should also bring two of every living thing of all flesh according to their kind. Noah got right to work and he put on his armor and gathered all the materials he needed to develop a filing system to maintain his records. He used metal to sharpen the pencil, papyrus plant for a notebook and he calculated his animals for food and income. Noah couldn't wait to use all those tools, because the Lord had determined to send rain on the earth for forty days, blotting out all living things He created. But, remember, God made a covenant with Noah and as a result of that covenant, Noah put his trust in the Lord. God inspired Noah to have a positive attitude. As Noah gathered the supplies and tools, God instructed him to complete his task of building the ark and gathering the appropriate number of animals and supplies.

The Right Tools

As a good steward, you should equip yourself with the right armor and put on your best walking shoes. Now, and for the next six days, begin to collect these items, and on the seventh day, reward yourself by resting for all the work you have done.

ITEMS NEEDED

1. Pencils—Needed for writing your daily monthly expenses.

2. Hanging File Folders—Needed for receipts and important statements.

3. Stapler—Needed for attaching your canceled check to your monthly statements.

4. File Cabinet—Needed for filing important paperwork.

5. Small Notebook—Needed for your thirty-day financial challenge to see where your money is being spent wisely or on unnecessary items.

6. Calculator—Needed to calculate your expenses quickly.

7. Paycheck Stub—Needed to do a cash flow analysis.

The Right File Cabinet

As a good steward, put on your breastplate and secure your file cabinet in a good location. The next thing you need to do is start organizing all your bills and statements for the next six days and on the seventh day, reward yourself with some rest.

1. Label the first hanging folder "Pay Stubs" and place your pay stubs in it for the next twelve months.

2. Label the second hanging folder "Savings Account." This information will show you how much was saved or spent.

3. Label the third hanging folder "Checking Account." Place your canceled checks inside the folder. This information will show your cash outflow.

4. Label the fourth hanging folder "Credit Cards." In it, put a separate folder for each monthly credit card statement to get a realistic view of how much debt you have.

5. Label the fifth hanging folder "ATM Receipts." This information will show you how m a n y times a month you withdrew cash and paid a transaction fee.

6. Label the sixth hanging folder "Other Liabilities." Create a folder for each debt, mortgage, cars, etc. This is very important when you are calculating your net worth.

7. Label the seventh hanging folder "Monthly Budget Worksheet." This will show you if you are making the right spending decision. Use the worksheet on page 12 and place inside this folder when finished.

8. Label the eighth hanging folder "Tax Returns." This provides income information and itemized deductions. Put seven file folders in the hanging folder, one for each year as a rule. You should keep old tax records for at least seven years in case the IRS wants to audit you. Genesis 2 (NIV) states, "By the seventh day God had finished the work he had been doing and he rested, blessed and made it Holy."

That's it, saints. You may discover that you are missing some statements, that's okay. Simply commit yourself for the next seventy-two hours to track down the information to complete your financial picture and when you have obtained a document, check it off under "Found" and place it in the proper folder. In the proper hanging folder, use the Missing Documents Worksheet on the next page to complete this task.

MISSING DOCUMENTS WORKSHEET

Missing Document	Location	Found
1. Example : Tax Return	Call IRS	
2.		
3.		
4.		
5.		
6.		
7.		
8.		
9.		

You now have completed and placed your financial documents in order. As a good steward for this assignment, reward yourself with some rest and prepare for the next challenge.

Date Completed _____

Your Signature _____

The Right Notebook

As a good steward, use your notebook for your thirty-day challenge, which is the shield, and begin tracking your everyday spending habits. Every Christian should operate with a budget to be the best steward for God. Begin to take your notebook everywhere you go for thirty days, starting tomorrow. Proverbs 24:3 (NIV) states, "By wisdom a house is built and by understanding it is established." Remember, habits change slowly. I want you to record all your money spent for the next thirty days. Write down every purchase you make, no matter what it is (coffee, candy, clothes, etc.). Perhaps you won't be able to write down the information immediately, but you do need to record the information before you go to bed.

Keep this thirty-day financial challenge for at least three months to determine a realistic spending pattern. You cannot put a budget into effect until this information is analyzed. Once you get into the habit of recording your financial expenses, it will gradually become easier. Let's start the process of annotating your wants and needs. Use The Thirty-Day Financial Challenge Worksheet on the next page as an example for your notebook. Record the total in the Want column and place that amount on Line 6 of your Monthly Budget Workhseet found on page 12 to help pay down your debt.

THE THIRTY-DAY FINANCIAL CHALLENGE WORKSHEET

Day	Item	Cost	Need	Want
1.				
2.				
3.				
4.				
5.				
6.				
7.				
8.				
9.				
10.				
11.				
12.				
Etc.				
			TOTAL:	

Additional worksheets can be found in the Index.

After the thirty days are up, total your "Wants" column. You now have a visual document of the amount of money you are wasting each month. That money can now be used to decrease your outstanding debt shown on #6 of your Monthly Budget Worksheet found on page 12. As you start noting your spending expenses, you'll see a pattern that can help you gauge and prepare for a positive financial budget.

The Right Calculator

As a good steward, your strong belt is to calculate your monthly budget expenses and to see if you have a positive cash flow. Every Christian needs to understand how much they spend. It's vitally important that you do a cash flow analysis to identify where you are financially. It can also help you make the right spending decision and have available money to save. It's so simple; all you have to do is subtract your monthly expenses from your monthly income. Hebrews 13:5 says, "Let your conduct be without covetousness, be content with such things as you have." Now, if you have some money left over, then you have a positive cash flow. However, if your expenses exceed your income, you have a negative cash flow. Proverbs 8:18 says, "There is one who makes himself rich, yet has nothing, and one who makes himself poor, yet has great riches."

Christians, if you fall in the negative cash flow, you cannot continue to be living above your means. 1 Timothy 6:17 states, "Command those who are rich in this present age not be haughty, nor to trust in uncertain riches, but in the living God, who gives us richly all things to enjoy." Use your Monthly Budget Worksheet on page 12 to determine if you have a positive cash flow. Put the extra money toward your savings and emergency cash fund on line 13.

Additional monthly budget worksheets can be found in the index section.

Circle Negative or Positive

Add lines 2 through 10 to sum your "Total Expenses" and then subtract line 11 from 12 to see if you have a positive cash flow. Put that total on line 14. Congratulations, if you have positive cash flow. If not, make necessary adjustments.

Note: Line 13—Do not use; only if an emergency.

MONTHLY BUDGET WORKSHEET

(1) Net salary   _____
     Net salary spouse   _____
     Other   _____
        Total Income _____

(2) Expenses
     Mortgage/Rent   _____
     Insurance   _____
     Taxes   _____
     Electricity   _____
     Gas   _____
     Water   _____
     Sanitation   _____
     Telephone   _____
     Maintenance   _____
     Other   _____

(3) Food   _____

(4) Clothing   _____

(5) Automobile
     Payment   _____
     Gas/Oil   _____
     Insurance   _____
     Maintenance   _____
     Other   _____

(6) Debts
     Credit Cards   _____
     Loans   _____
     Tithes   _____

(7) School   _____
     Tuition   _____
     Material   _____
     Trans.*   _____
     Day Care   _____

(8) Medical
     Doctor   _____
     Dentist   _____
     Insurance   _____

(9) Miscellaneous   _____
     Beauty   _____
     Barber   _____
     Laundry   _____
     Gifts   _____
     Other   _____

(10) Entertainment
     Dining   _____
     Movies   _____
     Plays   _____
     Other   _____

(11) Total Expenses _____

(12) Net Income   _____

(13) Savings Total
     Emergency Cash   _____
     Other   _____

(14) Total Income   _____

Transportation.

The Right Paycheck Stub

As a good steward, you need your paycheck stub to figure out how much money is being deducted from your gross salary. It is unbelievable to see how much money is being taken out for federal, state, local taxes, medical, retirement, etc. It is important to have ten percent systematically withheld from your paycheck so you can pay your tithes. Malachi 3:8 (NIV) asks a question: "Will a mere mortal rob God? Yet you rob me. But you ask, 'How are we robbing you?' In tithes and offerings.."

The Bible teaches us to be a faithful tither; your financial obligation is to honor God with the first ten percent of your earnings into the storehouse. By giving back to God's kingdom, He will multiply it back to you many times over as a result of all your deductions. Your actual take-home pay is called your net salary. On the next page, complete your Income Analysis Worksheet. You will need your latest paycheck stub. This figure doesn't tell you how much you spend, but is an important start for every budget. On the next page, you will analyze all the money you have deducted from your paycheck.

INCOME ANALYSIS WORKSHEET
MONTHLY CASH INCOME
TAKE-HOME PAY

(1) Income   _____   Income Spouse   _____

Self-employment Income   _____   Self-employment Income   _____

Bonus   _____   Bonus   _____

Commissions   _____   Commissions   _____

Other   _____   Other   _____

Total Income   _____

Employer Deductions

(2) Health insurance   _____

Life insurance   _____

Pension contributions   _____

401(k) Plan   _____

Other   _____

Total Benefits   _____

Tax Liabilities

(3) Federal income   _____

Social Security   _____

State income   _____

Other   _____

Total Liabilities   _____

Income from line (1)   _____

Add total Benefits from line (2)   _____

Add total Tax Liabilities line (3)   _____

Add lines (2) and (3), and subtract
    amount from line (1)   _____

This is your net salary   _____

Put your net salary on line (1) on your Monthly Budget Worksheet found on page 12.

Bonus Report

How to Have $1,000 in Your Pocket by the Evening!

Christians, if you find that you need additional income, no problem. What you must realize is God has given you time and with that time is another revenue for income. Don't just budget your money, budget your time. Your time is your money. Proverbs 10:45 (NIV) states, "Lazy hands make a man poor, but diligent hands bring wealth." Now! Follow this easy plan to make some additional income. It's called, "Street Corner Retailing." Lots of money has been made this way. Street Corner Retailing can be truly profitable if you are an outgoing person and like people. You do not need a lot of money to start your initial inventory or buy your merchandise and products. Remember, "Sluggards do not plow in season; so at harvest time they look but find nothing," Proverbs 20:4 (NIV). Christians, don't be a sluggard, don't wait until you need more money for a debt that you created; start now by increasing your income. Here are five examples to start making money.

(1) Yard Sale

(2) Sell Socks and Clothing

(3) Sell Handmade Crafts

(4) Handyman Work

(5) House Sitting

CHAPTER 3
Begin Saving

"Plan to Save for Financial Prosperity"

7 Good Reasons to Have a Budget

1. Allows you to pay yourself first.
2. Helps you to set realistic goals.
3. Teaches you to pay your bills on time.
4. Plan to live within your means.
5. You can start saving for your retirement.
6. Develop a positive cash flow.
7. Establish an emergency cash fund.

BEGIN SAVING

NOTES:

_____

_____

_____

_____

_____

_____

_____

_____

_____

_____

_____

_____

_____

_____

_____

_____

_____

_____

_____

_____

_____

_____

_____

_____

_____

_____

_____

Sow $3.65 a Day

Are you willing to save? One of God's greatest gifts that He gave us is time. As Christians, we are expected to use it wisely and to our advantage in fulfilling our financial goals. In 2 Corinthians 9:6 (NIV), remember this, "Whoever sows sparingly will also reap sparingly and whoever sows generously will also reap generously." Psalm 118:24 states, "This is the day which the Lord hath made, rejoice and be glad in it." According to the calendar year, there are three hundred sixty-five days. Every day God wakes you up, bless yourself by putting away $3.65 a day. Proverbs 23:4 (NIV) reminds us, "Do not wear yourself out to get rich; have wisdom to show restraint." But, before we jump right into saving $3.65 a day, let's look at the power of saving $3.65.

Day:	1	7	14	28	35
$ Saved:	3.65	25.55	51.10	102.20	127.75

Deposited Daily

Interest 5%

Okay, hopefully, I've motivated you. Genesis 2:3 (NIV), "And God blessed the seventh day and made it Holy, because on it he rested from all the work of creating that he had done." Start soon to begin saving $3.65 a day and annually put the money into a CD, Money Market or IRA and after seven years, enjoy the fruit of your labor. Right now, you should be motivated to sign this contract found on page 19 between you and God to pay yourself $3.65 a day.

Contract

I, [insert name], hereby, according to Numbers 30:2: "When a man makes a vow to the Lord or takes an oath to obligate himself by a pledge, he must not break his word, but must do everything he said," I promise God that I will begin paying myself three dollars and sixty-five cents a day no later than [insert date].

Signed _____   _____

               Name   God

This contract is important; you will find a copy of it in the index section. Make copies of it and place it in a location where you can see it every day, in places such as: the phone, refrigerator door, bathroom mirror, etc.

Good luck!

7 Years of Advanced Preparation

Genesis 41:49 (NIV) states, "During the seven years of abundance the land produced plentifully." Joseph collected all the food produced in those seven years of abundance in Egypt and stored it in the cities. In each city, he put the food grown in the fields surrounding it. Joseph stored up huge quantities of grain, like the sand of the sea. It was so much that he stopped keeping record, because it was beyond measure. The moral of this story is when you begin to sow you will reap the blessings. Below, write your seven years of advanced preparation.

_____

_____

_____

_____

_____

_____

_____

_____

_____

_____

_____

_____

_____

_____

_____

_____

_____

_____

_____

_____

Grocery Shopping Strategies

As a good steward, before going grocery shopping, take an inventory of your cabinet and refrigerator and make a list of items you need. Remember, supermarkets are usually designed to make money. Scriptural principles give us counsel as to how we can manage our money to be an effective shopper. You should plan, budget, and have self-control. Proverb 24:14 (NIV) reads, "Know also that wisdom is sweet to your soul." Christians, by using grocery store coupons, you can save some money and purchase extra items.

Here are a few tips next time you go grocery shopping.

☐ Be aware of supermarket traps. Higher priced goods are usually in the middle aisles.

☐ Be aware of products placed on sale at every aisle.

☐ Be aware of eye-level products. Look down and you will find a bargain.

☐ Check your Sunday newspaper for coupon specials.

☐ Purchase your shampoo, soap, toothpaste, and deodorant at a discount drug store.

Remember, (Hebrews 10:35 (NIV)), "So do not throw away your confidence, it will be richly rewarded.

(Make every dollar count.)

Use your grocery list work sheet on page 22 to list items needed.

GROCERY LIST WORKSHEET

Item	Coupons	Need	Want
1.			
2.			
3.			
4.			
5.			
7.			
8.			
9.			
10.			
11.			
12.			
13.			
14.			
15.			
16.			
17.			
18.			
19.			
20.			
21.			
22.			
23.			
24.			
25.			
26.			
27.			
28.			
29.			
30.			
31.			
32.			
33.			

Bonus Report

Save up to 50% Interest on Your Credit Card

Christians, it's vitally important to save on credit card interest and not be trapped into a high-interest account and annual fees. Proverbs 3:5-6 (KJV) states, "Trust in the Lord with all thine heart; and lean not unto thine own understanding. In all thy ways acknowledge him, and he shall direct thy paths." By utilizing this information, you can position yourself as a good steward and trade in your high-interest cards and save hundreds of dollars a year on the outstanding balances. Here is a list of companies I recommend, because of their no- or low-interest and annual fees. To get started, review your credit card statement and figure out how much you are paying on interest and annual fees and record your information in the worksheet on the next page. Below is a list of contact numbers that will provide information about saving interest on your credit cards. On page 24, record your new credit card information on the Debt Listing Worksheet.

(1)	Chase Freedom Unlimited (800) 432-3117	(6)	Citi Diamond Preferred (800) 950-5114
(2)	Discover it Cash Back (800) 347-2683	(7)	Wells Fargo Cash Wise Visa (800) 642-4720
(3)	Capital One Quicksilver Cash Rewards (800) 227-4825	(8)	Citi Simplicity (855) 860-2460
(4)	BankAmericard (800) 847-2911	(9)	Capital One SavorOne Cash Rewards (844) 788-8999
(5)	Bank of America Cash Rewards (800) 434-8313	(10)	Blue Cash Everyday from American Express (800) 528-4800

DEBT LISTING WORKSHEET

Debt Name	Annual Fees ($)	Interest (%)	Replace With (%)	Company Name	Phone Number
Example: Visa	$30.00	19.5	6.5	AFBA	800-555-1212
1.					
2.					
3.					
4.					
5.					
6.					
7.					
8.					
9.					
10.					
11.					
12.					
13.					
14.					
15.					
16.					
17.					
18.					
19.					
20.					
21.					
22.					
23.					
24.					
25.					
26.					
27.					
28.					
29.					
30.					

CHAPTER 4
Managing Your Spending Expenses

"It's time to start managing your spending expenses."

7 Good Reasons to Track Your Spending

1. You'll find out if you are splurging each month.
2. You'll find out where all your money is going.
3. You can visualize if you are making the right budgeting decisions.
4. You will find out where the cash you withdrew from the bank account is going.
5. You can stop unnecessary spending.
6. You will be able to be in control of your financial future.
7. You will be able to invest or save.

Analyze Expenses

Analyzing your expense comes in the form of three categories: Fixed, Variable and Discretionary Expenses. As you start to analyze your expenses, you'll notice some amount remains the same while other bills are different. For example, your rent, car payment, and loans will remain the same every month and are called your fixed expenses.

Expenses that you pay irregularly, such as your utility bills, food, clothing, and necessities are your variable expenses.

Finally, the third type of expense is called discretionary expenses, which is money spent at a barbershop, a beauty salon, car expenses, and non-essential items, like a bridal shower, baby shower, entertainment, and holiday gifts. Remember, to be a good steward, you have to account for all of your money.

MANAGING YOUR SPENDING EXPENSES

NOTES:

_____
_____
_____
_____
_____
_____
_____
_____
_____
_____
_____
_____
_____
_____
_____
_____
_____
_____
_____
_____
_____
_____
_____
_____
_____
_____
_____
_____
_____
_____
_____
_____
_____
_____

Tracking Monthly Expenses

Where does your money really go? Like many Christians, you probably don't know, not exactly anyway. There's your car payment, utility bills, car insurance, entertainment, buying gifts, and, of course, eating out, but what is really happening to the rest of your money from your paycheck?

To find out, you will need the records of your Monthly Budget Worksheet, which you have been annotating for one to three months. See page 12. It's important to account for every money spent on your fixed expenses, variable expenses, and discretionary expenses. Christians who said tracking your expenses will be easy, but it can make a difference to your financial budget.

As you start noting your spending expenses from your Monthly Budget Worksheet, you'll see a pattern that can help you gauge and prepare for a positive financial budget. Now start with your Monthly Budget Worksheet (see page 12) and transfer that amount to your Monthly Fixed Expenses found on page 29.

Tracking Fixed Expenses

Programming your thinking for tracking your fixed expenses is easy. Each day you must go to your mailbox and retrieve your monthly statement. The first thing you should do is open up your bills and see which one has a fixed amount. If you have a car payment, for example, simply review your coupon payment book to see how much you pay. Each month, annotate that amount on the Fixed Expense Worksheet found on page 29. Remember, you must start your days with faith, believing all your bills will get paid. Don't be surprised if you hear a voice in your mind saying, *This is a waste of time, nothing good is going to come out of this, you might as well continue how you've been paying your bills.* Don't listen; God wants you to prosper. The Bible says, "Faith is the substance of things hoped for." Set your financial budgeting expectations high starting today. Expect your change in attitude to be in your favor. It's that simple.

FIXED EXPENSES WORKSHEET

Expenses	Monthly
(1) Housing	
Rent	_____
Car Payment	_____
Home Mortgage	_____
Boat House	_____
RV Housing	_____
Total Fixed Housing Expenses	_____
(2) Insurance	_____
(3) Other Fixed Expenses	_____
Total	_____

Additional worksheets can be found in the Index.

Unanticipated Expenses

Christians, don't give up yet! Your budget is the blueprint for your financial success. Unfortunately, this is the last category that must be addressed. Your unanticipated expenses are eating away at your income. As good stewards, you need to set aside a sum of money to draw from to pay for a vacation, home improvement, professional fees, taxes, appliance repairs, car repair and, most importantly, medical. This will prevent you from using your credit cards or making a loan, which could put you in a bigger debt and your financial budget in ruins.

Finally, how do you prepare for these unanticipated expenses? Start by making a list of every foreseeable expense for the year. Assign an annual amount to each expense. Then divide by twelve to come up with a monthly amount. Use the Unanticipated Expenses Worksheet found on page 30 and set that money aside for upcoming expenses.

*Important: Put the amount on your Monthly Budget Worksheet found on page 12 on line 13 where it reads "others."

UNANTICIPATED EXPENSES WORKSHEET

Saving for Unanticipated Expenses	Amount Needed	Divided by 12	Amount to be Saved Per Month
Example: **Take a Vacation**	**$1,200.00**	**÷ 12**	**$100.00**
Home Improvement			
Professional Fees			
Mortgage Taxes			
Personal Taxes			
Appliance Repairs			
Car Repairs			
Medical			
Others			
1.			
2.			
3.			
4.			
5.			
6.			
7.			
8.			
		TOTAL	$

Additional workseets can be found in the Index.

Assign Your Variable Expenses

The next assignment is to list your variable expenses. The Bible says, in Hebrews 11:6 (NIV), "But without faith it is impossible to please him; for he that cometh to God must believe that he is, and that he is a rewarder of the that diligently seek him." But what is that? First, faith means that we believe God will provide. You, as a Christian, must have faith that when you list your variable expenses it will get paid; not tomorrow, no maybe, but as soon as you put it in the hands of God. Philippians 4:19 (NIV) says, "And my God will meet all your needs according to the riches of his glory in Christ Jesus." Remember, filling out this Variable Expenses Worksheet will take some time and effort on your part.

Review your billing statement and your Thirty-Day Financial Challenge Notebook you've been using to track your expenses for three months and list those items on the Variable Expenses Worksheet found on page 32. The items listed under each heading found on your Variable Expense Worksheet are to guide you—add or delete to reflect your values. As you create your list, think about what expenses can be reduced or eliminated so you can have a positive budgeting plan.

Your Final Result

So how are you doing? We're almost there, just a few more calculations and you will see your final results. There are three directions your cash flow analysis information can render. Matthew 13:16 (NIV) says, "Blessed are your eyes, because they see; and your ears, because they hear." God is extremely interested in how you visualize your budgeting plan. By seeing your plan, you will be able to make the right adjustment. If you have a positive cash flow, that means your income exceeds your expenses, you won't have to make any changes in your spending habits. However, if your income is about equal to your expenses, you are living within your means, you will need to reduce your expenses, start with non-necessity items so that you can have a little more money to save.

Finally, if you spend more than your net salary, you can fix this problem by eliminating your wants or apply for a part-time job. But, if you are not focusing or serious about your finances, you run the risk of going in the wrong direction and missing out on the great financial blessing God wants to give you. Write down your total monthly budget expenses and income on page 12 from your Monthly Budget Worksheet. The result is your cash flow, if you have a negative cash flow. We'll show you how to fix the problem in the following chapters, but if you have a positive cash flow, keep up the good work, saint.

VARIABLE EXPENSES WORKSHEET

* Use this worksheet with your thirty-day challenge.

Day	Month #1	Cost	Reduce	Month #2	Cost	Reduced	Eliminated
	Ex.: Coffee	$7.00					$7.00
1.							
2.							
3.							
4.							
5.							
6.							
7.							
8.							
9.							
10.							
11.							
12.							
13.							
14.							
15.							

Total $7.00 $7.00

Great! Saints, put these totals you have eliminated toward your emergency savings. On your Monthly Budget Worksheet found on page 12, line 13.

FINAL MONTHLY BUDGET WORKSHEET

	MONTH 1	MONTH 2
(1) Write your Total Monthly Income here from page 12 line 12	$	$
(2) Write your Total Monthly Expenses here from page 12 line 11	$	$
Subtract Line (2) from (1) … (If this is a negative cash flow, take action immediately.)	$	$
(3) Write your Total Emergency Savings here from page 12 line 13 (Congratulations! Keep up the good work on saving.)	$	$

Bonus Report

The Secret to Saving 10%

The secret to saving is to make use of what is known as, "The One Percent Solution." This method, together with the wonders of compound interest, can make you rich.

How it Works

The method does nothing less than make your ultimate goal. Here is how it works.

Step 1. Starting with your next paycheck, save one percent from each paycheck you receive in the next two months. So, if your weekly check is for $750, save $7.50 (one percent) every payday. That's right, just $7.50. After a few weeks, you won't even miss the $7.50. Open an interest-paying bank account in which to save the money each week.

Step 2. After two months, raise the amount by one percent so that you now save two percent, (an additional $7.50 for a total of $15.00 in our example). You'll feel like you only have $7.50 less to spend each week because you are now accustomed to the first $7.50.

Step 3. Now, repeat this procedure every two months so that you keep raising your savings by one percent until you reach a savings rate of ten percent. This will be your ultimate savings goal.

Congratulations, Saints!

It's time to build up your credit.

CHAPTER 5
Understanding Your Credit

"Build credit while saving money."

Credit Resolution

Here is the good news. If there are negative errors found on your credit report, for example, missed payments, charge-off, repossession, collection, student loans default, Chapter 7 Bankruptcy, and foreclosures, etc., the Federal Trade Commission (FTC) says after seven years the items must be removed except Chapter 13, which will stay on your file for ten years.

Deuteronomy 15:1, (1) at the end of every seven years you must cancel debts, (2) this is the manner of remission, every creditor shall cancel what he has loaned to his neighbor.

Today, let's focus on six easy steps for repairing and raising your FICO score.

Step 1

Sign up for the frce crcdit app at www.creditkarma.com or www.creditsesame.com to gauge where your FICO score is and to get a glimpse of what's on your credit report.

*Note: I have no affiliation with Credit Karma or Credit Sesame. I use both of these apps; they are great tools to have for your arsenal to begin restructuring your creditworthiness and raising your FICO score higher.

Step 2

Get a free copy of your credit report from www.annualcreditreport.com (for the first year get all three credit reports from each credit agency bureau then rotate every three months for each credit report.) That way, you will have a written file and stay up-to-date for the rest of the following years.

*Important: If you find errors on your credit file, send out the Dispute Letter to original creditors on page 43 to get supporting documents.

*Note: It is important to contact the credit reporting agency to see if they changed their guidelines.

TransUnion	Equifax	Experian
800-916-8800	800-685-1111	888-397-3742

Step 3

Dispute incorrect information. Once you get your credit report, let's start with your personal identification. It's common to see your name misspelled or a different name used and your social security number and address wrong.

Review your credit report for late payments, charge off, collection, judgment, bankruptcy, foreclosure, liens, etc. If you see any mistake or questionable items, highlight the errors and then use the form, Credit Report Errors on page 39 and take action.

Next, gather any information to back up your claim. Proof is important so the Credit Bureau can take your response seriously. Write a letter using the Credit Resolution Form found on page 40 to the specific credit agency who is reporting the falsehood on your report.

* Note: Send mail Certified so you can have a paper trail for all correspondence.

The reporting agency has thirty days from receipt of your letter to respond, but don't get discouraged as it may take up to one to five letters to get a final result.

Step 4

Contact the Federal Trade Commission (FTC) and begin the dispute on that credit agency if they are not responding to your letters.

Step 5

Raise your FICO score. Exodus 22:5 says, "If you lend money to my people, to the poor among you, you are not to act as a creditor to him, you shall not charge him interest." Hopefully, by now, you can see a pattern that the creditors and government are charging too much interest to borrow money and then you are punished with a bad reputation that can keep you from getting a job, housing, etc.

Now you must stop the bleeding. Fair Isaac and Company (FICO) is a data analytics company based in San Jose, California. Focus on credit scoring services. They determine your credit worthiness as follows: 35% payment history, 30% account owe, 15% length of credit, 10% inquires, 10% new credit.

Why is this so important? Knowledge is power. Let's begin to be a good religious, spiritual person and pay all of your bills on time. Pay down your debt and don't apply for no more credit cards or loans until you achieve your '800' FICO score. Good Luck!

Step 6

Build your credit. Take control and establish your credit: www.Self.Inc.com offers four different types of loans, each which you pay down monthly.

How it Works
Build Credit While Saving Money Starting at $25 per Month

Step 1

Apply for a loan that is held by their bank partner.

Step 2

Pay off the loan in 12—24 months; you choose a repayment plan.

Step 3

Each payment builds credit history and adds to your savings.

Step 4

Get money back at the end of the loan after building your credit history.

Victim of Identify Theft

Step 1

Contact your credit card company, Department of Motor Vehicles (DMV) and Social Security Department.

Step 2

File a Police Report and send it to the Credit Bureau Agency.

Step 3

File a complaint with the Federal Trade Commission (FTC).

Step 4

Notify one of the three credit agencies and they will forward the information to the other two credit agencies.

Legal Disclaimer: The content on this page just provides general consumer information. Contact the credit reporting agency's Fraud Alert Division for updated guidance.

Extended Fraud Alert Request Form

To place an Extended Fraud Alert on your credit report, please send via US Mail a valid, Police Report or Federal Trade Commission Identify Theft Report to:

1. Equifax Consumer Fraud Division   www.equifax.com/fraudalerts
   P.O. Box 740256
   Atlanta, GA 30374

2. Experian   www.experian.com/fraud/form
   P.O. Box 9554
   Allen, TX 75013

3. TransUnion Fraud Victim Assistance Dept.   www.TransUnion.com/fraudalerts
   P.O. Box 2000
   Chester, PA 19016

CREDIT REPORT ERROR FORM

UNDERSTANDING YOUR CREDIT

Acct. Name	Acct. #	Missed Payment	Charge Off	Repo	Bankruptcy Chapter 7 & 3	Student Loans	Foreclosure	Inquiry	Judgment	Tax	Comment
Visa	000-11										

Additional worksheets can be found in the Index.

CREDIT RESOLUTION FORM
Letters to Take Action

Card Type	Account Number	Report Errors	Follow Up	Dispute Mistake	Closing Account
1. Visa	00-111	1-2020 Experian		2-2020	
2.					
3.					
4.					
5.					
6.					
7.					
8.					
9.					
10.					
11.					
12.					
13.					
14.					
15.					
16.					
17.					
18.					
19.					
20.					

Additional worksheets can be found in the Index.

DISPUTE LETTER FOR FRAUDULENT CHARGES

Date

Your Name
Your Address
Your City, State, Zip Code
Your Account Number

Name of Creditor/Bank
Address
City, State, Zip Code

Dear Sir or Madam:

I am writing to dispute a fraudulent [charge or debit] on my account in the amount of $ _____.
I am a victim of Identify Theft, and I did not make this [charge or debit]. I am requesting that
the [charge be removed or the debit reinstated], that any finance and other charges related to the
fraudulent amount be credited, as well, and that I receive an accurate statement.

Enclosed are copies of [use this sentence to describe any enclosed information, such as a police
report] supporting my position. Please investigate this matter and correct the fraudulent [charge
or debit] as soon as possible. I would appreciate a response from you in writing. Thank you for
your assistance.

Sincerely,

[Your Name]

Enclosures: (List what you are enclosing)

SAMPLE DISPUTE LETTER TO ORIGINAL CREDITOR

Date

Your Name
Your Address
Your City, State, Zip Code

Name of Creditor
Address
City, State, Zip Code

Ref: Account #

Dear Sir or Madam:

I am writing to dispute the inaccurate information that your company is reporting to (Example); TransUnion late payment. According to the FCRA, Section 623 it's your company's responsibility to furnish correct information.

I dispute your information in its entirety and request evidentiary documentation. Should you not be able or willing to provide me with substantiating documentation within the next thirty (30) days, please have the information deleted from each of the Credit Reporting Agencies you furnish.

Thank you very much,

Your Name

DISPUTE LETTER 1 SAMPLE

Send this letter first with a copy of your credit report highlighting the inaccurate errors you found.

Date

Your First and Last Name
Your Address
Your City, State, Zip Code

Experian
P.O. Box 9701
Allen, TX 75013

Re: Inaccurate and Errors Found

To Whom It May Concern:

I am writing to dispute the following information in my file. The items in dispute are encircled on the attached copy of the report I received.

The items I am disputing are as follow:

Example
1. Account number 1111-111 never late
2. Account number 1111- never had a Charge Off

I am requesting that the items be corrected.

Enclosed are copies of supporting documentation. Please investigate this matter and correct these disputed items as soon as possible.

Sincerely,

Your Name   DOB: _____
Phone Number: _____   Driver's License: _____

DISPUTE LETTER 2 FOLLOW-UP

The second letter should be sent out to the credit reporting agency if you did not get an answer after thirty (30) days. Send by Registered Mail and make sure the credit reporting address has not changed.

Your First and Last Name
Your Address
Your City, State, Zip Code

Date

Experian
P.O. Box 9701
Allen, TX 75013

Re: Second Request [Insert File Number]

To Whom It May Concern:

On [Insert Date of First Letter], I sent a Certified Letter requesting the errors be investigated and removed or corrected.

Example
1. Account number 1111-111 never late
2. Account number 1111- never had a Charge Off

According to the Fair Credit Reporting Act (FCRA), please honor my request within thirty (30) days and correct the above mention errors.

Sincerely,

Your Name   DOB: _____

Phone Number: Driver's License: _____

DISPUTE LETTER 3 MISTAKES

Use this letter to dispute any individual errors or inaccurate information that has been placed on your file.

Your First and Last Name
Your Address
Your City, State, Zip Code

Date

Experian
P.O. Box 9701
Allen, TX 75013

Re: Individual Errors

To Whom It May Concern:

I am writing to dispute the following error on my report file [Insert brief description of mistake made]. I have enclosed a copy of proof.

Account Number
Dispute Information
Correct Dispute

Please provide me with the correction accordance with the Fair Credit Reporting Act (FCRA, Section 168 (1)).

Sincerely,

Your Name   DOB: _____

Phone Number: Driver's License: _____

CLOSING OPEN ACCOUNTS

Your First and Last Name
Your Address
Your City, State, Zip Code

Date

Name of Credit Agency
Address
City, State, Zip Code

Re: Requesting to Close Open Accounts

To Whom It May Concern:

After reviewing my credit report file [Insert file number], Date _____.

Upon discovering account #[   ] is still open, please correct the account reference above.

I have enclosed a copy of the letter sent to the original credit agency closing the account.

Sincerely,

Your Name   DOB: _____

Phone Number: Driver's License: _____

REQUEST LETTER TO CREDITOR TO CLOSE THE ACCOUNT

Your First and Last Name
Your Address
Your City, State, Zip Code

Date

Name of Creditors
Address
City, State, Zip Code

Re: Immediate Cancellation of My Account
    [Insert account number]

To Whom It May Concern:

I recently reviewed my credit report [Insert File Number and Date], it is currently open.

Please close this account immediately and report it to the Reporting Credit Agency [Insert Agency Name].

Sincerely,

Your Name   Cell Number: _____

Bonus Report

Increase Your Credit Score 50 Points

Step 1	Do not close old account
Step 2	Pay down credit card at least half the amount
Step 3	Do not apply for new credit
Step 4	Make payment on time
Step 5	Use your credit card responsibly
Step 6	Raising your credit limit
Step 7	Limit inquiries

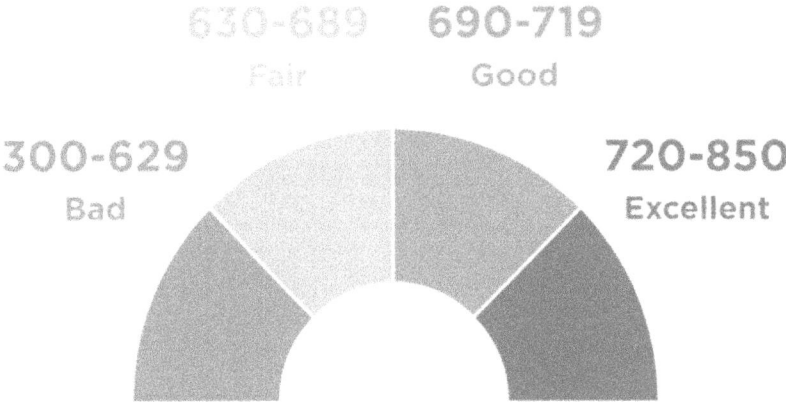

Almost There, Saints!

CHAPTER 6
Debt Collection Practice

"Make a plan and stay in control."

Now spiritual Saints, you made it this far, I'm proud of you (keep up the good work). Matthew 21-22 says, if you believe, you will receive whatever you ask for in prayer. It's time to stop the creditors from harassment. Matthew 6:12 says, and forgive us our debts, as we also have forgiven our debtors. Its true Saints that we ask God to forgive our debts and in the process of forgiving our debtors. Now the Federal Fair Debt Collection Practice Act (FDCPA) is the law that we must use to stop creditors from intimidating and harassment.

It's illegal for debt collectors to do the following.

☐ Contact your employer (unless they have a lawsuit to garnish your wages)

☐ Call at unreasonable hours (they can call between 8 AM to 9 PM)

☐ Use derogatory or insulting language

☐ Call repeatedly

☐ Call without disclosing identity

It is your legal right to stop the harassment until you work out a payment plan to honor your debts.

Now in the process, if you have been violated, you may sue the credit collection agency for damage and attorney fees.

Follow these easy steps to stop the credit agency from contacting you, but it's your obligation to pay them.

Remember they still have the right to report a negative remark on your credit file; now let's began the process of contacting the credit agency to stop the harassment.

Step 1

Send out the sample (cease and desist) collection letter to the collection agency that is harassing you.

Step 2

Send out the same letter, but include how they are intimidating you. Send to:

Federal Trade Commission
600 Pennsylvania Avenue, NW
Washington, DC 20850

Step 3

If the harassment doesn't stop, hire an attorney.

Step 4

File for bankruptcy, usually the initial paperwork will protect you from collection activity.

Note: Contact a bankruptcy attorney for final consultation. (I am not a lawyer to be giving legal advice).

NOTES:

_____

_____

_____

_____

_____

_____

_____

_____

_____

_____

_____

_____

_____

_____

_____

_____

_____

_____

_____

_____

_____

_____

_____

_____

_____

DEBT RELIEF OPTIONS

1. It can be stressful, but the first action is open up all unpaid bills.
2. Create a Game Plan and contact the creditor by calling, they should work with you.
3. Ask the creditors to schedule a new repayment plan.
4. If you have a mortgage, ask what your options are.
5. Get help with a Certified Credit Counselor.
6. Consolidate your loans for a lower monthly loan.
7. Student loans, contact the lender for options that are available.

SAMPLE CEASE AND DESIST LETTER

Date

Your First and Last Name
Address
City, State, Zip Code

Re: Account Number

To Whom It May Concern:

According to my rights under federal debt collection laws, I am requesting that you cease and desist communication with me, as well as my job in relation to this and all other alleged debts you claim I owe.

You are hereby notified that if you do not comply with this request, I will immediately file a complaint with the Federal Trade Commission and the [Your state here] Attorney General's Office, Civil and Criminal.

Sincerely,

Your Name

SAMPLE LETTER OF UNRECOGNIZED DEBT

Use this letter if you don't recognize a debt or mailing you received.

Date

Your First and Last Name
Address
City, State, Zip Code

Debt Collector's Name
Address

Re: Account Number

Dear [Debt Collector's Name]:
   I am responding to your contact about a debt you are trying to collect. You contacted me by [Phone/Mail] on [Date] and identified the debt as [Any information they gave you about the debt].

   Please supply the information below so that I can be fully informed.

- ☐ The name and address of the original creditor and amount owed.
- ☐ Verification and documentation that there is a valid basis for claiming that I am required to pay the debt to the current creditor.

The amount and age of the debt, including:

- ☐ A copy of the last billing statement sent to me by the original creditor.
- ☐ State the amount of the debt when you obtained.
- ☐ Does your firm have a debt collection license for my state?

I have asked for this information, because I have some questions.

Please let me know whether your company will accept less than the balance you claim is owed.

Sincerely,

[Your Name]

SAMPLE DISPUTE AND PROOF LETTER

Your Name
Address
City, State, Zip Code

Date

Debt Collector Name
Address
City, State, Zip Code

Re: Account

Dear [Debt Collector Name]

I am responding to your contact about collecting a debt. You contacted me by [Phone/Mail], on [Date] and identified the debt as [any information they gave you about the debt].

I do not have any responsibility for the debt you are trying to collect.

If you have good reason to believe this is my debt, send me all supporting documentation.

If you stop your collection of this debt and forward or return it to another company, please indicate to them that it is disputed. If you report it to a credit bureau [or have already done so], also report that the debt is disputed.

Sincerely,

[Your Name]

SAMPLE CONTACT MY ATTORNEY

If a Lawyer is representing you about a debt, send this letter to the debt collector.
*Note: After you have sent this letter, the debt collector should not contact you unless the Lawyer is not responding.

Your Name
Address
City, State, Zip Code

Date

Debt Collector Name
Address
City, State, Zip Code

Re: Account

To Whom It May Concern:

I am responding to your contact about the collection of a debt. You contacted me by [Phone/Mail] on [Date] and identified the debt as [any information they gave you about the debt].

Please contact my lawyer about this debt, and do not contact me directly again. My lawyer's contact information is:

[Contact information for your lawyer]

Sincerely,

[Your Name]

SAMPLE LETTER HOW TO CONTACT ME

*Note: Use this sample letter to tell a debt collector how to contact you.

Your Name
Address
City, State, Zip Code

Date

Debt Collector Name
Address
City, State, Zip Code

Re: Account

I am responding to your contact about collecting a debt. Your company contacted me by [Phone/ Mail] on [Date] and identified the debt as [any information they gave you about the debt].

You can contact me about this debt, but only in the way I say below. Don't contact me about this debt in other way or at any other place of time.

I authorize you to contact me at:

[Mailing address if you want to get mail]
[Phone number time to be contacted]
[Not at work]

Thank you for your cooperation.

Sincerely,

[Your Name]

Congratulations!

I pray that all the hard work you have put in using these financial tools have helped to get your finances back on track and your debts eliminated.

CHAPTER 7
Computerizing Your Finances

"Using a computer is easier than ever."

Financial Software

If you own a computer, managing your budget will become easier in the future. There are many personal financial software on the market: Microsoft Money, Quicken, etc.

How can the software benefit you? They'll help you in the following area:

- ☐ Review past spending
- ☐ Record all expenses
- ☐ Calculate all expenditures
- ☐ Project future spending
- ☐ Intelligently calculate debt reduction
- ☐ Manage your money

Christians, it's important to take control of your money and learn all about the options the software has to offer, beginning with you and your family; a new pattern of using the computer and apps to simplify your finances and wealth. Ecclesiastes 3:1 says, "To everything there is a season, and a time to every purpose under the Heaven."

Using the Internet

Many of your financial budgeting information can be found by using the Internet. You'll find hundreds of sites on budget planning, credit cards, savings and budgeting software.

Savings and tips, in addition you can use the Internet to communicate with expert financial planners.

As you search the web, you will learn how easy it is to locate budgeting articles to help you save some money every month.

This information site has numerous articles about budgeting. Take a look at www.kiplinger. com. It has a free calculator that can help you figure out how much money to save for retirement and how long it will take to pay off your credit card debt to meet your budget goals. Next, go to www.bankrate.com and www.bestrate.com, where you will find competitive lower interest rates on credit cards. The Budget Site Worksheet found on page 63 will help you maintain a list of all the websites you visit by placing a check mark in the proper category, you can visualize what sites you visited.

To get started on your search, go to any search engine (i.e., Google.com) and type in www. smartaboutmoney.org.

On-Line Budgeting

Managing your finances and budget can be time consuming and stressful at times, but don't worry, here are a list of websites that can help you track spending, create and manage budgets, and reports.

(1) www.mint.com

This budget software has security encryption that help track your budget, credit score and investment.

(2) www.acemoneylite.com

Helps track your finance in multiple currencies and spending habits as well as on-line banking.

(3) www.personalcapital.com

Helps you plan for retirement, analyze your cash flow, spending and net worth.

BUDGETING SITES WORKSHEET

Location	Budget Planning	Credit Cards	Budget Software	Saving Tips
www.saving.com				
1.				
2.				
3.				
4.				
5.				
6.				
7.				
8.				
9.				
10.				
11.				
12.				

Index

The forms included in this section are important, print them and make additional copies as needed.

MISSING DOCUMENTS WORKSHEET

Missing Document	Location	Found
1. Example :Tax Return	Call IRS	
2.		
3.		
4.		
5.		
6.		
7.		
8.		
9.		

MONTHLY BUDGET WORKSHEET

(1) Net salary   _____   (7) School   _____
     Net salary spouse   _____   Tuition   _____
     Other   _____   Material   _____
       Total Income   _____   Trans.*   _____
     Day Care   _____

(2) Expenses
     Mortgage/Rent   _____   (8) Medical
     Insurance   _____   Doctor   _____
     Taxes   _____   Dentist   _____
     Electricity   _____   Insurance   _____
     Gas   _____
     Water   _____   (9) Miscellaneous   _____
     Sanitation   _____   Beauty   _____
     Telephone   _____   Barber   _____
     Maintenance   _____   Laundry   _____
     Other   _____   Gifts   _____
     Other   _____

(3) Food   _____
     (10) Entertainment
(4) Clothing   _____   Dining   _____
     Movies   _____
(5) Automobile   Plays   _____
     Payment   _____   Other   _____
     Gas/Oil   _____
     Insurance   _____   (11) Total Expenses   _____
     Maintenance   _____
     Other   _____   (12) Net Income   _____

(6) Debts   (13) Savings Total
     Credit Cards   _____   Emergency Cash   _____
     Loans   _____   Other   _____
     Tithes   _____
     (14) Total Income   _____

Transportation.

THE THIRTY-DAY FINANCIAL CHALLENGE WORKSHEET

Day	Item	Cost	Need	Want
1.				
2.				
3.				
4.				
5.				
6.				
7.				
8.				
9.				
10.				
11.				
12.				
Etc.				
			TOTAL:	

UNANTICIPATED EXPENSES WORKSHEET

Saving for Unanticipated Expenses	Amount Needed	Divided by 12	Amount to be Saved Per Month
Example: **Take a Vacation**	**$1,200.00**	**÷ 12**	**$100.00**
Home Improvement			
Professional Fees			
Mortgage Taxes			
Personal Taxes			
Appliance Repairs			
Car Repairs			
Medical			
Others			
1.			
2.			
3.			
4.			
5.			
6.			
7.			
8.			
TOTAL	$		

Additional workseets can be found in the Index.

CREDIT REPORT ERROR FORM

Acct. Name	Acct. #	Missed Payment	Charge Off	Repo	Bankruptcy Chapter 7 & 3	Student Loans	Foreclosure	Inquiry	Judgment	Tax	Comment
Visa	000-11										

CREDIT RESOLUTION FORM
Letters to Take Action

Card Type	Account Number	Report Errors	Follow Up	Dispute Mistake	Closing Account
1. Visa	00-111	1-2020 Experian		2-2020	
2.					
3.					
4.					
5.					
6.					
7.					
8.					
9.					
10.					
11.					
12.					
13.					
14.					
15.					
16.					
17.					
18.					
19.					
20.					

FIXED EXPENSES WORKSHEET

Expenses	Monthly
(1) Housing	
Rent	_____
Car Payment	_____
Home Mortgage	_____
Boat House	_____
RV Housing	_____
Total Fixed Housing Expenses	_____
(2) Insurance	_____
(3) Other Fixed Expenses	_____
Total	_____

Contract

I, [insert name], hereby, according to Numbers 30:2: "When a man makes a vow to the Lord or takes an oath to obligate himself by a pledge, he must not break his word, but must do everything he said," I promise God that I will begin paying myself three dollars and sixty-five cents a day no later than [insert date].

Signed _____   _____
                  Name   God

Cut out this contract on the dotted line and put it in a location where you can see it every day. Example: phone, refrigerator door, bathroom mirror, etc.

Good luck!

Contract

I, [insert name], hereby, according to Numbers 30:2: "When a man makes a vow to the Lord or takes an oath to obligate himself by a pledge, he must not break his word, but must do everything he said," I promise God that I will begin paying myself three dollars and sixty-five cents a day no later than [insert date].

Signed _____   _____

                Name   God

Cut out this contract on the dotted line and put it in a location where you can see it every day. Example: phone, refrigerator door, bathroom mirror, etc.

Good luck!